Table of Contents

Name _____

School _____

Grade/Subject _____

Room _____

School Year _____

Address _____

Phone _____

Teacher Created Resources
12621 Western Avenue
Garden Grove, CA 92841
www.teachercreated.com
ISBN: 978-1-4206-8295-3
©2019 Teacher Created Resources
Reprinted, 2019
Made in U.S.A.

Editor in Chief: Karen Goldfluss, M.S. Ed.

Creative Director: Sarah M. Fournier

Cover Design: Denise Bauer

Publisher: Mary D. Smith, M.S. Ed.

Teacher Created Resources

Monthly Reminders (page 3)

Use this chart as a quick reference. Record significant events and upcoming meetings, appointments, conferences, seminars, etc.

Student Roster (pages 4-5)

Record both student and parent or guardian names and addresses. Where applicable, make a special note of differences in last names. You may wish to list siblings and their grades if they attend the same school. Notes may include information regarding special needs children and medications necessary.

Weekly Records (pages 6-63)

The weekly record section is designed to provide organized space for recording daily notations or grades for assignments, tests, attendance, tardies, participation, etc. Each page contains a five-week block of spaces so that a student's record for an entire quarter of ten weeks can be read on facing pages. Summary columns for recording total attendance, tardies, and other information appear on the right-hand facing page for each ten-week period.

Grading Chart (page 64)

A convenient chart for scoring students' work is provided at the back of this book. Use the chart as a quick reference when scoring 3 to 50 items of equal value. To use the chart, simply "connect" the row that matches the total number of items to be scored with the column indicating the number of incorrect items.

By following across the row and up the column to the intersection point (number), you can determine the raw score. For example, if the total number of items on a given test is 35, and a student marked 5 incorrectly, his or her score would be 86%. The score is obtained by moving across row 35 and up column 5 to the point where they meet (86%).

Grading Chart

Monthly Reminders

AUGUST

Date	Notes

SEPTEMBER

Date	Notes

OCTOBER

Date	Notes

NOVEMBER

Date	Notes

DECEMBER

Date	Notes

JANUARY

Date	Notes

FEBRUARY

Date	Notes

MARCH

Date	Notes

APRIL

Date	Notes

MAY

Date	Notes

JUNE

Date	Notes

JULY

Date	Notes

	STUDENT	PARENT/GUARDIAN	ADDRESS
1.			
2.			
3.			
4.			
5.			
6.			
7.			
8.			
9.			
10.			
11.			
12.			
13.			
14.			
15.			
16.			
17.			
18.			
19.			
20.			
21.			
22.			
23.			
24.			
25.			
26.			
27.			
28.			
29.			
30.			
31.			
32.			
33.			
34.			
35.			
36.			

Roster

WORK & HOME PHONES	SIBLINGS	NOTES

Subject _____ Time/Period _____	Assignments	Week					Week					Week					Week					Week				
NAME / Day Date		M	T	W	T	F	M	T	W	T	F	M	T	W	T	F	M	T	W	T	F	M	T	W	T	F
	1																									
	2																									
	3																									
	4																									
	5																									
	6																									
	7																									
	8																									
	9																									
	10																									
	11																									
	12																									
	13																									
	14																									
	15																									
	16																									
	17																									
	18																									
	19																									
	20																									
	21																									
	22																									
	23																									
	24																									
	25																									
	26																									
	27																									
	28																									
	29																									
	30																									
	31																									
	32																									
	33																									
	34																									
	35																									
	36																									

Week					Week					Week					Week					Week						Days Present	Days Absent	Tardies		
M	T	W	T	F	M	T	W	T	F	M	T	W	T	F	M	T	W	T	F	M	T	W	T	F	1					
																									2					
																									3					
																									4					
																									5					
																									6					
																									7					
																									8					
																									9					
																									10					
																									11					
																									12					
																									13					
																									14					
																									15					
																									16					
																									17					
																									18					
																									19					
																									20					
																									21					
																									22					
																									23					
																									24					
																									25					
																									26					
																									27					
																									28					
																									29					
																									30					
																									31					
																									32					
																									33					
																									34					
																									35					
																									36					

Subject _____ Time/Period _____	Assignments		Week					Week					Week					Week					Week				
NAME	Day / Date	M	T	W	T	F	M	T	W	T	F	M	T	W	T	F	M	T	W	T	F	M	T	W	T	F
	1																									
	2																									
	3																									
	4																									
	5																									
	6																									
	7																									
	8																									
	9																									
	10																									
	11																									
	12																									
	13																									
	14																									
	15																									
	16																									
	17																									
	18																									
	19																									
	20																									
	21																									
	22																									
	23																									
	24																									
	25																									
	26																									
	27																									
	28																									
	29																									
	30																									
	31																									
	32																									
	33																									
	34																									
	35																									
	36																									

Week					Week					Week					Week					Week						Days Present	Days Absent	Tardies		
M	T	W	T	F	M	T	W	T	F	M	T	W	T	F	M	T	W	T	F	M	T	W	T	F	1					
																									2					
																									3					
																									4					
																									5					
																									6					
																									7					
																									8					
																									9					
																									10					
																									11					
																									12					
																									13					
																									14					
																									15					
																									16					
																									17					
																									18					
																									19					
																									20					
																									21					
																									22					
																									23					
																									24					
																									25					
																									26					
																									27					
																									28					
																									29					
																									30					
																									31					
																									32					
																									33					
																									34					
																									35					
																									36					

Subject ___ Time/Period ___	Assignments	Week					Week					Week					Week					Week				
NAME	Day / Date	M	T	W	T	F	M	T	W	T	F	M	T	W	T	F	M	T	W	T	F	M	T	W	T	F
	1																									
	2																									
	3																									
	4																									
	5																									
	6																									
	7																									
	8																									
	9																									
	10																									
	11																									
	12																									
	13																									
	14																									
	15																									
	16																									
	17																									
	18																									
	19																									
	20																									
	21																									
	22																									
	23																									
	24																									
	25																									
	26																									
	27																									
	28																									
	29																									
	30																									
	31																									
	32																									
	33																									
	34																									
	35																									
	36																									

Week					Week					Week					Week					Week						Days Present	Days Absent	Tardies			
M	T	W	T	F	M	T	W	T	F	M	T	W	T	F	M	T	W	T	F	M	T	W	T	F							
																									1						
																									2						
																									3						
																									4						
																									5						
																									6						
																									7						
																									8						
																									9						
																									10						
																									11						
																									12						
																									13						
																									14						
																									15						
																									16						
																									17						
																									18						
																									19						
																									20						
																									21						
																									22						
																									23						
																									24						
																									25						
																									26						
																									27						
																									28						
																									29						
																									30						
																									31						
																									32						
																									33						
																									34						
																									35						
																									36						

Subject _____ Time/Period _____	Assignments	Week					Week					Week					Week					Week				
NAME	Day / Date	M	T	W	T	F	M	T	W	T	F	M	T	W	T	F	M	T	W	T	F	M	T	W	T	F
	1																									
	2																									
	3																									
	4																									
	5																									
	6																									
	7																									
	8																									
	9																									
	10																									
	11																									
	12																									
	13																									
	14																									
	15																									
	16																									
	17																									
	18																									
	19																									
	20																									
	21																									
	22																									
	23																									
	24																									
	25																									
	26																									
	27																									
	28																									
	29																									
	30																									
	31																									
	32																									
	33																									
	34																									
	35																									
	36																									

Week					Week					Week					Week					Week						Days Present	Days Absent	Tardies		
M	T	W	T	F	M	T	W	T	F	M	T	W	T	F	M	T	W	T	F	M	T	W	T	F							
																									1					
																									2					
																									3					
																									4					
																									5					
																									6					
																									7					
																									8					
																									9					
																									10					
																									11					
																									12					
																									13					
																									14					
																									15					
																									16					
																									17					
																									18					
																									19					
																									20					
																									21					
																									22					
																									23					
																									24					
																									25					
																									26					
																									27					
																									28					
																									29					
																									30					
																									31					
																									32					
																									33					
																									34					
																									35					
																									36					

Subject _____ Time/Period _____	Assignments	Week					Week					Week					Week					Week				
NAME / Day Date		M	T	W	T	F	M	T	W	T	F	M	T	W	T	F	M	T	W	T	F	M	T	W	T	F
	1																									
	2																									
	3																									
	4																									
	5																									
	6																									
	7																									
	8																									
	9																									
	10																									
	11																									
	12																									
	13																									
	14																									
	15																									
	16																									
	17																									
	18																									
	19																									
	20																									
	21																									
	22																									
	23																									
	24																									
	25																									
	26																									
	27																									
	28																									
	29																									
	30																									
	31																									
	32																									
	33																									
	34																									
	35																									
	36																									

Week					Week					Week					Week					Week						Days Present	Days Absent	Tardies			
M	T	W	T	F	M	T	W	T	F	M	T	W	T	F	M	T	W	T	F	M	T	W	T	F							
																									1						
																									2						
																									3						
																									4						
																									5						
																									6						
																									7						
																									8						
																									9						
																									10						
																									11						
																									12						
																									13						
																									14						
																									15						
																									16						
																									17						
																									18						
																									19						
																									20						
																									21						
																									22						
																									23						
																									24						
																									25						
																									26						
																									27						
																									28						
																									29						
																									30						
																									31						
																									32						
																									33						
																									34						
																									35						
																									36						

Subject _____ Time/Period _____	Assignments	Week					Week					Week					Week					Week				
NAME	Day / Date	M	T	W	T	F	M	T	W	T	F	M	T	W	T	F	M	T	W	T	F	M	T	W	T	F
	1																									
	2																									
	3																									
	4																									
	5																									
	6																									
	7																									
	8																									
	9																									
	10																									
	11																									
	12																									
	13																									
	14																									
	15																									
	16																									
	17																									
	18																									
	19																									
	20																									
	21																									
	22																									
	23																									
	24																									
	25																									
	26																									
	27																									
	28																									
	29																									
	30																									
	31																									
	32																									
	33																									
	34																									
	35																									
	36																									

Week					Week					Week					Week					Week						Days Present	Days Absent	Tardies			
M	T	W	T	F	M	T	W	T	F	M	T	W	T	F	M	T	W	T	F	M	T	W	T	F	1						
																									2						
																									3						
																									4						
																									5						
																									6						
																									7						
																									8						
																									9						
																									10						
																									11						
																									12						
																									13						
																									14						
																									15						
																									16						
																									17						
																									18						
																									19						
																									20						
																									21						
																									22						
																									23						
																									24						
																									25						
																									26						
																									27						
																									28						
																									29						
																									30						
																									31						
																									32						
																									33						
																									34						
																									35						
																									36						

NAME	Day Date	Week M T W T F	Week M T W T F	Week M T W T F	Week M T W T F	Week M T W T F
	1					
	2					
	3					
	4					
	5					
	6					
	7					
	8					
	9					
	10					
	11					
	12					
	13					
	14					
	15					
	16					
	17					
	18					
	19					
	20					
	21					
	22					
	23					
	24					
	25					
	26					
	27					
	28					
	29					
	30					
	31					
	32					
	33					
	34					
	35					
	36					

Subject

Time/Period

Assignments

Week					Week					Week					Week					Week						Days Present	Days Absent	Tardies		
M	T	W	T	F	M	T	W	T	F	M	T	W	T	F	M	T	W	T	F	M	T	W	T	F	1					
																									2					
																									3					
																									4					
																									5					
																									6					
																									7					
																									8					
																									9					
																									10					
																									11					
																									12					
																									13					
																									14					
																									15					
																									16					
																									17					
																									18					
																									19					
																									20					
																									21					
																									22					
																									23					
																									24					
																									25					
																									26					
																									27					
																									28					
																									29					
																									30					
																									31					
																									32					
																									33					
																									34					
																									35					
																									36					

Subject _____ Time/Period _____	Assignments	Week					Week					Week					Week					Week				
NAME / Day Date		M	T	W	T	F	M	T	W	T	F	M	T	W	T	F	M	T	W	T	F	M	T	W	T	F
	1																									
	2																									
	3																									
	4																									
	5																									
	6																									
	7																									
	8																									
	9																									
	10																									
	11																									
	12																									
	13																									
	14																									
	15																									
	16																									
	17																									
	18																									
	19																									
	20																									
	21																									
	22																									
	23																									
	24																									
	25																									
	26																									
	27																									
	28																									
	29																									
	30																									
	31																									
	32																									
	33																									
	34																									
	35																									
	36																									

Week					Week					Week					Week					Week							Days Present	Days Absent	Tardies			
M	T	W	T	F	M	T	W	T	F	M	T	W	T	F	M	T	W	T	F	M	T	W	T	F								
																									1							
																									2							
																									3							
																									4							
																									5							
																									6							
																									7							
																									8							
																									9							
																									10							
																									11							
																									12							
																									13							
																									14							
																									15							
																									16							
																									17							
																									18							
																									19							
																									20							
																									21							
																									22							
																									23							
																									24							
																									25							
																									26							
																									27							
																									28							
																									29							
																									30							
																									31							
																									32							
																									33							
																									34							
																									35							
																									36							

Subject	Assignments	Week					Week					Week					Week					Week				
Time/Period																										

NAME	Day / Date	M	T	W	T	F	M	T	W	T	F	M	T	W	T	F	M	T	W	T	F	M	T	W	T	F
	1																									
	2																									
	3																									
	4																									
	5																									
	6																									
	7																									
	8																									
	9																									
	10																									
	11																									
	12																									
	13																									
	14																									
	15																									
	16																									
	17																									
	18																									
	19																									
	20																									
	21																									
	22																									
	23																									
	24																									
	25																									
	26																									
	27																									
	28																									
	29																									
	30																									
	31																									
	32																									
	33																									
	34																									
	35																									
	36																									

Week					Week					Week					Week					Week						Days Present	Days Absent	Tardies		
M	T	W	T	F	M	T	W	T	F	M	T	W	T	F	M	T	W	T	F	M	T	W	T	F	1					
																									2					
																									3					
																									4					
																									5					
																									6					
																									7					
																									8					
																									9					
																									10					
																									11					
																									12					
																									13					
																									14					
																									15					
																									16					
																									17					
																									18					
																									19					
																									20					
																									21					
																									22					
																									23					
																									24					
																									25					
																									26					
																									27					
																									28					
																									29					
																									30					
																									31					
																									32					
																									33					
																									34					
																									35					
																									36					

Subject _____ Time/Period _____	Assignments	Week					Week					Week					Week					Week				
NAME	Day / Date	M	T	W	T	F	M	T	W	T	F	M	T	W	T	F	M	T	W	T	F	M	T	W	T	F
	1																									
	2																									
	3																									
	4																									
	5																									
	6																									
	7																									
	8																									
	9																									
	10																									
	11																									
	12																									
	13																									
	14																									
	15																									
	16																									
	17																									
	18																									
	19																									
	20																									
	21																									
	22																									
	23																									
	24																									
	25																									
	26																									
	27																									
	28																									
	29																									
	30																									
	31																									
	32																									
	33																									
	34																									
	35																									
	36																									

Week					Week					Week					Week					Week					Days Present	Days Absent	Tardies			
M	T	W	T	F	M	T	W	T	F	M	T	W	T	F	M	T	W	T	F	M	T	W	T	F						
																									1					
																									2					
																									3					
																									4					
																									5					
																									6					
																									7					
																									8					
																									9					
																									10					
																									11					
																									12					
																									13					
																									14					
																									15					
																									16					
																									17					
																									18					
																									19					
																									20					
																									21					
																									22					
																									23					
																									24					
																									25					
																									26					
																									27					
																									28					
																									29					
																									30					
																									31					
																									32					
																									33					
																									34					
																									35					
																									36					

NAME	Day Date	Week M	T	W	T	F	Week M	T	W	T	F	Week M	T	W	T	F	Week M	T	W	T	F	Week M	T	W	T	F
	1																									
	2																									
	3																									
	4																									
	5																									
	6																									
	7																									
	8																									
	9																									
	10																									
	11																									
	12																									
	13																									
	14																									
	15																									
	16																									
	17																									
	18																									
	19																									
	20																									
	21																									
	22																									
	23																									
	24																									
	25																									
	26																									
	27																									
	28																									
	29																									
	30																									
	31																									
	32																									
	33																									
	34																									
	35																									
	36																									

Subject

Time/Period

Assignments

Week					Week					Week					Week					Week						Days Present	Days Absent	Tardies			
M	T	W	T	F	M	T	W	T	F	M	T	W	T	F	M	T	W	T	F	M	T	W	T	F							
																									1						
																									2						
																									3						
																									4						
																									5						
																									6						
																									7						
																									8						
																									9						
																									10						
																									11						
																									12						
																									13						
																									14						
																									15						
																									16						
																									17						
																									18						
																									19						
																									20						
																									21						
																									22						
																									23						
																									24						
																									25						
																									26						
																									27						
																									28						
																									29						
																									30						
																									31						
																									32						
																									33						
																									34						
																									35						
																									36						

Subject _____ Time/Period _____	Assignments	Week					Week					Week					Week					Week				

NAME	Day / Date	M	T	W	T	F	M	T	W	T	F	M	T	W	T	F	M	T	W	T	F	M	T	W	T	F
	1																									
	2																									
	3																									
	4																									
	5																									
	6																									
	7																									
	8																									
	9																									
	10																									
	11																									
	12																									
	13																									
	14																									
	15																									
	16																									
	17																									
	18																									
	19																									
	20																									
	21																									
	22																									
	23																									
	24																									
	25																									
	26																									
	27																									
	28																									
	29																									
	30																									
	31																									
	32																									
	33																									
	34																									
	35																									
	36																									

Week					Week					Week					Week					Week						Days Present	Days Absent	Tardies			
M	T	W	T	F	M	T	W	T	F	M	T	W	T	F	M	T	W	T	F	M	T	W	T	F							
																									1						
																									2						
																									3						
																									4						
																									5						
																									6						
																									7						
																									8						
																									9						
																									10						
																									11						
																									12						
																									13						
																									14						
																									15						
																									16						
																									17						
																									18						
																									19						
																									20						
																									21						
																									22						
																									23						
																									24						
																									25						
																									26						
																									27						
																									28						
																									29						
																									30						
																									31						
																									32						
																									33						
																									34						
																									35						
																									36						

Subject _____ Time/Period _____	Assignments	Week					Week					Week					Week					Week				
NAME	Day / Date	M	T	W	T	F	M	T	W	T	F	M	T	W	T	F	M	T	W	T	F	M	T	W	T	F
	1																									
	2																									
	3																									
	4																									
	5																									
	6																									
	7																									
	8																									
	9																									
	10																									
	11																									
	12																									
	13																									
	14																									
	15																									
	16																									
	17																									
	18																									
	19																									
	20																									
	21																									
	22																									
	23																									
	24																									
	25																									
	26																									
	27																									
	28																									
	29																									
	30																									
	31																									
	32																									
	33																									
	34																									
	35																									
	36																									

Week					Week					Week					Week					Week						Days Present	Days Absent	Tardies			
M	T	W	T	F	M	T	W	T	F	M	T	W	T	F	M	T	W	T	F	M	T	W	T	F	1						
																									2						
																									3						
																									4						
																									5						
																									6						
																									7						
																									8						
																									9						
																									10						
																									11						
																									12						
																									13						
																									14						
																									15						
																									16						
																									17						
																									18						
																									19						
																									20						
																									21						
																									22						
																									23						
																									24						
																									25						
																									26						
																									27						
																									28						
																									29						
																									30						
																									31						
																									32						
																									33						
																									34						
																									35						
																									36						

Subject _____ Time/Period _____	Assignments	Week					Week					Week					Week					Week				
NAME	Day / Date	M	T	W	T	F	M	T	W	T	F	M	T	W	T	F	M	T	W	T	F	M	T	W	T	F
	1																									
	2																									
	3																									
	4																									
	5																									
	6																									
	7																									
	8																									
	9																									
	10																									
	11																									
	12																									
	13																									
	14																									
	15																									
	16																									
	17																									
	18																									
	19																									
	20																									
	21																									
	22																									
	23																									
	24																									
	25																									
	26																									
	27																									
	28																									
	29																									
	30																									
	31																									
	32																									
	33																									
	34																									
	35																									
	36																									

Week					Week					Week					Week					Week						Days Present	Days Absent	Tardies		
M	T	W	T	F	M	T	W	T	F	M	T	W	T	F	M	T	W	T	F	M	T	W	T	F						
																									1					
																									2					
																									3					
																									4					
																									5					
																									6					
																									7					
																									8					
																									9					
																									10					
																									11					
																									12					
																									13					
																									14					
																									15					
																									16					
																									17					
																									18					
																									19					
																									20					
																									21					
																									22					
																									23					
																									24					
																									25					
																									26					
																									27					
																									28					
																									29					
																									30					
																									31					
																									32					
																									33					
																									34					
																									35					
																									36					

Subject _____ Time/Period _____	Assignments	Week					Week					Week					Week					Week				
NAME	Day / Date	M	T	W	T	F	M	T	W	T	F	M	T	W	T	F	M	T	W	T	F	M	T	W	T	F
	1																									
	2																									
	3																									
	4																									
	5																									
	6																									
	7																									
	8																									
	9																									
	10																									
	11																									
	12																									
	13																									
	14																									
	15																									
	16																									
	17																									
	18																									
	19																									
	20																									
	21																									
	22																									
	23																									
	24																									
	25																									
	26																									
	27																									
	28																									
	29																									
	30																									
	31																									
	32																									
	33																									
	34																									
	35																									
	36																									

Week					Week					Week					Week					Week						Days Present	Days Absent	Tardies		
M	T	W	T	F	M	T	W	T	F	M	T	W	T	F	M	T	W	T	F	M	T	W	T	F							
																									1					
																									2					
																									3					
																									4					
																									5					
																									6					
																									7					
																									8					
																									9					
																									10					
																									11					
																									12					
																									13					
																									14					
																									15					
																									16					
																									17					
																									18					
																									19					
																									20					
																									21					
																									22					
																									23					
																									24					
																									25					
																									26					
																									27					
																									28					
																									29					
																									30					
																									31					
																									32					
																									33					
																									34					
																									35					
																									36					

Subject	Assignments	Week					Week					Week					Week					Week				
Time/Period																										
NAME	Day / Date	M	T	W	T	F	M	T	W	T	F	M	T	W	T	F	M	T	W	T	F	M	T	W	T	F
	1																									
	2																									
	3																									
	4																									
	5																									
	6																									
	7																									
	8																									
	9																									
	10																									
	11																									
	12																									
	13																									
	14																									
	15																									
	16																									
	17																									
	18																									
	19																									
	20																									
	21																									
	22																									
	23																									
	24																									
	25																									
	26																									
	27																									
	28																									
	29																									
	30																									
	31																									
	32																									
	33																									
	34																									
	35																									
	36																									

Week					Week					Week					Week					Week						Days Present	Days Absent	Tardies			
M	T	W	T	F	M	T	W	T	F	M	T	W	T	F	M	T	W	T	F	M	T	W	T	F							
																									1						
																									2						
																									3						
																									4						
																									5						
																									6						
																									7						
																									8						
																									9						
																									10						
																									11						
																									12						
																									13						
																									14						
																									15						
																									16						
																									17						
																									18						
																									19						
																									20						
																									21						
																									22						
																									23						
																									24						
																									25						
																									26						
																									27						
																									28						
																									29						
																									30						
																									31						
																									32						
																									33						
																									34						
																									35						
																									36						

Subject _____ Time/Period _____	Assignments		Week				Week				Week				Week				Week			
NAME	Day / Date		M	T	W	T	F	M	T	W	T	F	M	T	W	T	F	M	T	W	T	F	M	T	W	T	F
	1																					
	2																					
	3																					
	4																					
	5																					
	6																					
	7																					
	8																					
	9																					
	10																					
	11																					
	12																					
	13																					
	14																					
	15																					
	16																					
	17																					
	18																					
	19																					
	20																					
	21																					
	22																					
	23																					
	24																					
	25																					
	26																					
	27																					
	28																					
	29																					
	30																					
	31																					
	32																					
	33																					
	34																					
	35																					
	36																					

Week					Week					Week					Week					Week					Days Present	Days Absent	Tardies				
M	T	W	T	F	M	T	W	T	F	M	T	W	T	F	M	T	W	T	F	M	T	W	T	F							
																									1						
																									2						
																									3						
																									4						
																									5						
																									6						
																									7						
																									8						
																									9						
																									10						
																									11						
																									12						
																									13						
																									14						
																									15						
																									16						
																									17						
																									18						
																									19						
																									20						
																									21						
																									22						
																									23						
																									24						
																									25						
																									26						
																									27						
																									28						
																									29						
																									30						
																									31						
																									32						
																									33						
																									34						
																									35						
																									36						

Subject _____ Time/Period _____	Assignments	Week					Week					Week					Week					Week				
NAME	Day / Date	M	T	W	T	F	M	T	W	T	F	M	T	W	T	F	M	T	W	T	F	M	T	W	T	F
	1																									
	2																									
	3																									
	4																									
	5																									
	6																									
	7																									
	8																									
	9																									
	10																									
	11																									
	12																									
	13																									
	14																									
	15																									
	16																									
	17																									
	18																									
	19																									
	20																									
	21																									
	22																									
	23																									
	24																									
	25																									
	26																									
	27																									
	28																									
	29																									
	30																									
	31																									
	32																									
	33																									
	34																									
	35																									
	36																									

Week					Week					Week					Week					Week						Days Present	Days Absent	Tardies			
M	T	W	T	F	M	T	W	T	F	M	T	W	T	F	M	T	W	T	F	M	T	W	T	F							
																									1						
																									2						
																									3						
																									4						
																									5						
																									6						
																									7						
																									8						
																									9						
																									10						
																									11						
																									12						
																									13						
																									14						
																									15						
																									16						
																									17						
																									18						
																									19						
																									20						
																									21						
																									22						
																									23						
																									24						
																									25						
																									26						
																									27						
																									28						
																									29						
																									30						
																									31						
																									32						
																									33						
																									34						
																									35						
																									36						

Subject _____ Time/Period _____	Assignments	Week					Week					Week					Week					Week				
NAME — Day / Date		M	T	W	T	F	M	T	W	T	F	M	T	W	T	F	M	T	W	T	F	M	T	W	T	F
	1																									
	2																									
	3																									
	4																									
	5																									
	6																									
	7																									
	8																									
	9																									
	10																									
	11																									
	12																									
	13																									
	14																									
	15																									
	16																									
	17																									
	18																									
	19																									
	20																									
	21																									
	22																									
	23																									
	24																									
	25																									
	26																									
	27																									
	28																									
	29																									
	30																									
	31																									
	32																									
	33																									
	34																									
	35																									
	36																									

Week					Week					Week					Week					Week						Days Present	Days Absent	Tardies				
M	T	W	T	F	M	T	W	T	F	M	T	W	T	F	M	T	W	T	F	M	T	W	T	F									
																									1								
																									2								
																									3								
																									4								
																									5								
																									6								
																									7								
																									8								
																									9								
																									10								
																									11								
																									12								
																									13								
																									14								
																									15								
																									16								
																									17								
																									18								
																									19								
																									20								
																									21								
																									22								
																									23								
																									24								
																									25								
																									26								
																									27								
																									28								
																									29								
																									30								
																									31								
																									32								
																									33								
																									34								
																									35								
																									36								

Subject _____ Time/Period _____	Assignments	Week					Week					Week					Week					Week				
NAME	Day / Date	M	T	W	T	F	M	T	W	T	F	M	T	W	T	F	M	T	W	T	F	M	T	W	T	F
	1																									
	2																									
	3																									
	4																									
	5																									
	6																									
	7																									
	8																									
	9																									
	10																									
	11																									
	12																									
	13																									
	14																									
	15																									
	16																									
	17																									
	18																									
	19																									
	20																									
	21																									
	22																									
	23																									
	24																									
	25																									
	26																									
	27																									
	28																									
	29																									
	30																									
	31																									
	32																									
	33																									
	34																									
	35																									
	36																									

#8295 Record Book | 44 | ©Teacher Created Resources

Week					Week					Week					Week					Week						Days Present	Days Absent	Tardies			
M	T	W	T	F	M	T	W	T	F	M	T	W	T	F	M	T	W	T	F	M	T	W	T	F							
																									1						
																									2						
																									3						
																									4						
																									5						
																									6						
																									7						
																									8						
																									9						
																									10						
																									11						
																									12						
																									13						
																									14						
																									15						
																									16						
																									17						
																									18						
																									19						
																									20						
																									21						
																									22						
																									23						
																									24						
																									25						
																									26						
																									27						
																									28						
																									29						
																									30						
																									31						
																									32						
																									33						
																									34						
																									35						
																									36						

Subject	Assignments	Week					Week					Week					Week					Week				
Time/Period																										
	Day	M	T	W	T	F	M	T	W	T	F	M	T	W	T	F	M	T	W	T	F	M	T	W	T	F
NAME	Date																									
	1																									
	2																									
	3																									
	4																									
	5																									
	6																									
	7																									
	8																									
	9																									
	10																									
	11																									
	12																									
	13																									
	14																									
	15																									
	16																									
	17																									
	18																									
	19																									
	20																									
	21																									
	22																									
	23																									
	24																									
	25																									
	26																									
	27																									
	28																									
	29																									
	30																									
	31																									
	32																									
	33																									
	34																									
	35																									
	36																									

Week					Week					Week					Week					Week						Days Present	Days Absent	Tardies		
M	T	W	T	F	M	T	W	T	F	M	T	W	T	F	M	T	W	T	F	M	T	W	T	F						
																									1					
																									2					
																									3					
																									4					
																									5					
																									6					
																									7					
																									8					
																									9					
																									10					
																									11					
																									12					
																									13					
																									14					
																									15					
																									16					
																									17					
																									18					
																									19					
																									20					
																									21					
																									22					
																									23					
																									24					
																									25					
																									26					
																									27					
																									28					
																									29					
																									30					
																									31					
																									32					
																									33					
																									34					
																									35					
																									36					

NAME	Day / Date	Week					Week					Week					Week					Week				
		M	T	W	T	F	M	T	W	T	F	M	T	W	T	F	M	T	W	T	F	M	T	W	T	F
	1																									
	2																									
	3																									
	4																									
	5																									
	6																									
	7																									
	8																									
	9																									
	10																									
	11																									
	12																									
	13																									
	14																									
	15																									
	16																									
	17																									
	18																									
	19																									
	20																									
	21																									
	22																									
	23																									
	24																									
	25																									
	26																									
	27																									
	28																									
	29																									
	30																									
	31																									
	32																									
	33																									
	34																									
	35																									
	36																									

Subject

_____

Time/Period

_____

Assignments

Week					Week					Week					Week					Week						Days Present	Days Absent	Tardies				
M	T	W	T	F	M	T	W	T	F	M	T	W	T	F	M	T	W	T	F	M	T	W	T	F								
																									1							
																									2							
																									3							
																									4							
																									5							
																									6							
																									7							
																									8							
																									9							
																									10							
																									11							
																									12							
																									13							
																									14							
																									15							
																									16							
																									17							
																									18							
																									19							
																									20							
																									21							
																									22							
																									23							
																									24							
																									25							
																									26							
																									27							
																									28							
																									29							
																									30							
																									31							
																									32							
																									33							
																									34							
																									35							
																									36							

Subject _____ Time/Period _____	Assignments	Week					Week					Week					Week					Week				
NAME	Day / Date	M	T	W	T	F	M	T	W	T	F	M	T	W	T	F	M	T	W	T	F	M	T	W	T	F
	1																									
	2																									
	3																									
	4																									
	5																									
	6																									
	7																									
	8																									
	9																									
	10																									
	11																									
	12																									
	13																									
	14																									
	15																									
	16																									
	17																									
	18																									
	19																									
	20																									
	21																									
	22																									
	23																									
	24																									
	25																									
	26																									
	27																									
	28																									
	29																									
	30																									
	31																									
	32																									
	33																									
	34																									
	35																									
	36																									

#8295 Record Book　　　　50　　　　©Teacher Created Resources

Week					Week					Week					Week					Week						Days Present	Days Absent	Tardies			
M	T	W	T	F	M	T	W	T	F	M	T	W	T	F	M	T	W	T	F	M	T	W	T	F	1						
																									2						
																									3						
																									4						
																									5						
																									6						
																									7						
																									8						
																									9						
																									10						
																									11						
																									12						
																									13						
																									14						
																									15						
																									16						
																									17						
																									18						
																									19						
																									20						
																									21						
																									22						
																									23						
																									24						
																									25						
																									26						
																									27						
																									28						
																									29						
																									30						
																									31						
																									32						
																									33						
																									34						
																									35						
																									36						

NAME	Day Date	M	T	W	T	F	M	T	W	T	F	M	T	W	T	F	M	T	W	T	F	M	T	W	T	F
	1																									
	2																									
	3																									
	4																									
	5																									
	6																									
	7																									
	8																									
	9																									
	10																									
	11																									
	12																									
	13																									
	14																									
	15																									
	16																									
	17																									
	18																									
	19																									
	20																									
	21																									
	22																									
	23																									
	24																									
	25																									
	26																									
	27																									
	28																									
	29																									
	30																									
	31																									
	32																									
	33																									
	34																									
	35																									
	36																									

Assignments — Week — Week — Week — Week — Week

Week					Week					Week					Week					Week						Days Present	Days Absent	Tardies		
M	T	W	T	F	M	T	W	T	F	M	T	W	T	F	M	T	W	T	F	M	T	W	T	F						
																									1					
																									2					
																									3					
																									4					
																									5					
																									6					
																									7					
																									8					
																									9					
																									10					
																									11					
																									12					
																									13					
																									14					
																									15					
																									16					
																									17					
																									18					
																									19					
																									20					
																									21					
																									22					
																									23					
																									24					
																									25					
																									26					
																									27					
																									28					
																									29					
																									30					
																									31					
																									32					
																									33					
																									34					
																									35					
																									36					

Subject _____ Time/Period _____	Assignments	Week					Week					Week					Week					Week				
NAME	Day / Date	M	T	W	T	F	M	T	W	T	F	M	T	W	T	F	M	T	W	T	F	M	T	W	T	F
	1																									
	2																									
	3																									
	4																									
	5																									
	6																									
	7																									
	8																									
	9																									
	10																									
	11																									
	12																									
	13																									
	14																									
	15																									
	16																									
	17																									
	18																									
	19																									
	20																									
	21																									
	22																									
	23																									
	24																									
	25																									
	26																									
	27																									
	28																									
	29																									
	30																									
	31																									
	32																									
	33																									
	34																									
	35																									
	36																									

Week					Week					Week					Week					Week						Days Present	Days Absent	Tardies		
M	T	W	T	F	M	T	W	T	F	M	T	W	T	F	M	T	W	T	F	M	T	W	T	F							
																									1					
																									2					
																									3					
																									4					
																									5					
																									6					
																									7					
																									8					
																									9					
																									10					
																									11					
																									12					
																									13					
																									14					
																									15					
																									16					
																									17					
																									18					
																									19					
																									20					
																									21					
																									22					
																									23					
																									24					
																									25					
																									26					
																									27					
																									28					
																									29					
																									30					
																									31					
																									32					
																									33					
																									34					
																									35					
																									36					

Subject _____ Time/Period _____	Assignments	Week					Week					Week					Week					Week				
NAME	Day / Date	M	T	W	T	F	M	T	W	T	F	M	T	W	T	F	M	T	W	T	F	M	T	W	T	F
	1																									
	2																									
	3																									
	4																									
	5																									
	6																									
	7																									
	8																									
	9																									
	10																									
	11																									
	12																									
	13																									
	14																									
	15																									
	16																									
	17																									
	18																									
	19																									
	20																									
	21																									
	22																									
	23																									
	24																									
	25																									
	26																									
	27																									
	28																									
	29																									
	30																									
	31																									
	32																									
	33																									
	34																									
	35																									
	36																									

Week					Week					Week					Week					Week						Days Present	Days Absent	Tardies		
M	T	W	T	F	M	T	W	T	F	M	T	W	T	F	M	T	W	T	F	M	T	W	T	F						
																									1					
																									2					
																									3					
																									4					
																									5					
																									6					
																									7					
																									8					
																									9					
																									10					
																									11					
																									12					
																									13					
																									14					
																									15					
																									16					
																									17					
																									18					
																									19					
																									20					
																									21					
																									22					
																									23					
																									24					
																									25					
																									26					
																									27					
																									28					
																									29					
																									30					
																									31					
																									32					
																									33					
																									34					
																									35					
																									36					

Subject _____ Time/Period _____	Assignments	Week					Week					Week					Week					Week				
NAME	Day / Date	M	T	W	T	F	M	T	W	T	F	M	T	W	T	F	M	T	W	T	F	M	T	W	T	F
	1																									
	2																									
	3																									
	4																									
	5																									
	6																									
	7																									
	8																									
	9																									
	10																									
	11																									
	12																									
	13																									
	14																									
	15																									
	16																									
	17																									
	18																									
	19																									
	20																									
	21																									
	22																									
	23																									
	24																									
	25																									
	26																									
	27																									
	28																									
	29																									
	30																									
	31																									
	32																									
	33																									
	34																									
	35																									
	36																									

Week					Week					Week					Week					Week						Days Present	Days Absent	Tardies		
M	T	W	T	F	M	T	W	T	F	M	T	W	T	F	M	T	W	T	F	M	T	W	T	F						
																									1					
																									2					
																									3					
																									4					
																									5					
																									6					
																									7					
																									8					
																									9					
																									10					
																									11					
																									12					
																									13					
																									14					
																									15					
																									16					
																									17					
																									18					
																									19					
																									20					
																									21					
																									22					
																									23					
																									24					
																									25					
																									26					
																									27					
																									28					
																									29					
																									30					
																									31					
																									32					
																									33					
																									34					
																									35					
																									36					

NAME	Day Date	Week					Week					Week					Week					Week				
		M	T	W	T	F	M	T	W	T	F	M	T	W	T	F	M	T	W	T	F	M	T	W	T	F
	1																									
	2																									
	3																									
	4																									
	5																									
	6																									
	7																									
	8																									
	9																									
	10																									
	11																									
	12																									
	13																									
	14																									
	15																									
	16																									
	17																									
	18																									
	19																									
	20																									
	21																									
	22																									
	23																									
	24																									
	25																									
	26																									
	27																									
	28																									
	29																									
	30																									
	31																									
	32																									
	33																									
	34																									
	35																									
	36																									

Subject

Time/Period

Assignments

Week					Week					Week					Week					Week						Days Present	Days Absent	Tardies			
M	T	W	T	F	M	T	W	T	F	M	T	W	T	F	M	T	W	T	F	M	T	W	T	F								
																									1						
																									2						
																									3						
																									4						
																									5						
																									6						
																									7						
																									8						
																									9						
																									10						
																									11						
																									12						
																									13						
																									14						
																									15						
																									16						
																									17						
																									18						
																									19						
																									20						
																									21						
																									22						
																									23						
																									24						
																									25						
																									26						
																									27						
																									28						
																									29						
																									30						
																									31						
																									32						
																									33						
																									34						
																									35						
																									36						

Subject

_____

Time/Period

_____

NAME	Day / Date	Week					Week					Week					Week					Week				
		M	T	W	T	F	M	T	W	T	F	M	T	W	T	F	M	T	W	T	F	M	T	W	T	F
	1																									
	2																									
	3																									
	4																									
	5																									
	6																									
	7																									
	8																									
	9																									
	10																									
	11																									
	12																									
	13																									
	14																									
	15																									
	16																									
	17																									
	18																									
	19																									
	20																									
	21																									
	22																									
	23																									
	24																									
	25																									
	26																									
	27																									
	28																									
	29																									
	30																									
	31																									
	32																									
	33																									
	34																									
	35																									
	36																									

Week					Week					Week					Week					Week						Days Present	Days Absent	Tardies		
M	T	W	T	F	M	T	W	T	F	M	T	W	T	F	M	T	W	T	F	M	T	W	T	F							
																									1					
																									2					
																									3					
																									4					
																									5					
																									6					
																									7					
																									8					
																									9					
																									10					
																									11					
																									12					
																									13					
																									14					
																									15					
																									16					
																									17					
																									18					
																									19					
																									20					
																									21					
																									22					
																									23					
																									24					
																									25					
																									26					
																									27					
																									28					
																									29					
																									30					
																									31					
																									32					
																									33					
																									34					
																									35					
																									36					

Grading Chart

Total Number of Items	1	2	3	4	5	6	7	8	9	10	11	12	13	14	15	16	17	18	19	20	21	22	23	24	25	26	27	28	29	30
50	98	96	94	92	90	88	86	84	82	80	78	76	74	72	70	68	66	64	62	60	58	56	54	52	50	48	46	44	42	40
49	98	96	94	92	90	88	86	84	82	80	78	76	73	71	69	67	65	63	61	59	57	55	53	51	49	47	45	43	41	39
48	98	96	94	92	90	88	85	83	81	79	77	75	73	71	69	67	65	63	60	58	56	54	52	50	48	46	44	42	40	38
47	98	96	94	91	89	87	85	83	81	79	77	74	72	70	68	66	64	62	60	57	55	53	51	49	47	45	43	40	38	36
46	98	96	93	91	89	87	85	81	80	78	76	74	72	70	67	65	63	61	59	57	54	52	50	48	46	43	41	39	37	35
45	98	95	93	91	89	87	84	82	80	78	76	73	71	69	67	64	62	60	58	56	53	51	49	47	44	42	40	38	36	33
44	98	95	93	91	89	86	84	82	80	77	75	73	70	68	66	64	61	59	57	55	52	50	48	45	43	41	39	36	34	32
43	98	95	93	91	88	86	84	81	79	77	74	72	70	67	65	63	60	58	56	53	51	49	47	44	42	40	37	35	33	30
42	98	95	93	90	88	86	83	81	79	76	74	71	69	67	64	62	60	57	55	52	50	48	45	43	40	38	36	33	31	29
41	98	95	93	90	88	85	83	80	78	75	73	71	68	66	63	61	59	56	54	51	49	46	44	41	39	37	34	32	29	27
40	98	95	93	90	88	85	83	80	78	75	73	70	68	65	63	60	58	55	53	50	48	45	43	40	38	35	33	30	28	25
39	97	95	92	90	87	85	82	79	77	74	72	69	67	64	62	59	56	54	51	49	46	44	41	38	36	33	31	28	26	23
38	97	95	92	89	87	84	82	79	76	74	71	68	66	63	61	58	55	53	50	47	45	42	39	37	34	32	29	26	24	21
37	97	95	92	89	86	84	81	78	76	73	70	68	65	62	59	57	54	51	49	46	43	41	38	35	32	30	27	24	22	19
36	97	94	92	89	86	83	81	78	75	72	69	67	64	61	58	56	53	50	47	44	42	39	36	33	31	28	25	22	19	17
35	97	94	91	89	86	83	80	77	74	71	69	66	63	60	57	54	51	49	46	43	40	37	34	31	29	26	23	20	17	14
34	97	94	91	88	85	82	79	76	74	71	68	65	62	59	56	53	50	47	44	41	38	35	32	39	26	24	21	18	15	12
33	97	94	91	88	85	82	79	76	73	70	67	64	61	58	55	52	48	45	42	39	36	33	30	27	24	21	18	15	12	9
32	97	94	91	88	84	81	78	75	72	69	66	63	59	56	53	50	47	44	41	38	34	31	28	25	22	19	16	13	9	6
31	97	94	90	87	84	81	77	74	71	68	65	61	58	55	52	48	45	42	39	35	32	29	26	23	19	16	13	10	6	3
30	97	93	90	87	83	80	77	73	70	67	63	60	57	53	50	47	43	40	37	33	30	27	23	20	17	13	10	7	3	
29	97	93	90	86	83	79	76	72	69	66	62	59	55	52	48	45	41	38	34	31	28	24	21	17	14	10	7	3		
28	96	93	89	86	82	79	75	71	68	64	61	57	54	50	46	43	39	36	32	29	25	21	18	14	11	7	4			
27	96	93	89	85	81	78	74	70	67	63	59	56	52	48	44	41	37	33	30	26	22	19	15	11	7	4				
26	96	92	88	85	81	77	73	69	65	62	58	54	50	46	42	38	35	31	27	23	19	15	12	8	4					
25	96	92	88	84	80	76	72	68	64	60	56	52	48	44	40	36	32	28	24	20	16	12	8	4						
24	96	92	88	83	79	75	71	67	63	58	54	50	46	42	38	33	29	25	21	17	13	8	4							
23	96	91	87	83	78	74	70	65	61	57	52	48	43	39	35	30	26	22	17	13	9	4								
22	95	91	86	82	77	73	68	64	59	55	50	45	41	36	32	27	23	18	14	9	5									
21	95	90	86	81	76	71	67	62	57	52	48	43	38	33	29	24	19	14	10	5										
20	95	90	85	80	75	70	65	60	55	50	45	40	35	30	25	20	15	10	5											
19	95	89	84	79	74	68	63	58	53	47	42	37	32	26	21	16	11	5												
18	94	89	83	78	72	67	61	56	50	44	39	33	28	22	17	11	6													
17	94	88	82	76	71	65	59	53	47	41	35	29	24	19	12	6														
16	94	88	81	75	69	63	56	50	44	38	31	25	19	13	6															
15	93	87	80	73	67	60	53	47	40	33	27	20	13	7																
14	93	86	79	71	64	57	50	43	36	29	21	14	7																	
13	92	85	77	69	62	54	46	38	31	23	15	8																		
12	92	83	75	67	58	50	42	33	25	17	8																			
11	91	82	73	64	55	45	36	27	18	9																				
10	90	80	70	60	50	40	30	20	10																					
9	89	78	67	56	44	36	22	11																						
8	88	75	63	50	38	25	13																							
7	86	71	57	43	29	14																								
6	83	67	50	33	17																									
5	80	60	40	20																										
4	75	50	25																											
3	67	33																												

Number of Incorrect Items